DK eyewonder
Volcanoes

LONDON, NEW YORK, MUNICH,
MELBOURNE, and DELHI

Written and edited by Lisa Magloff
Designed by Laura Roberts
Publishing manager Susan Leonard
Managing art editor Clare Shedden
Jacket editor Anna Stewart
Picture researcher Sarah Pownall
Production Shivani Pandey
DTP designer Almudena Díaz
Consultant Chris Pellant

REVISED EDITION
DK UK
Senior editor Caroline Stamps
Senior art editor Rachael Grady
Jacket design Natasha Rees
Producer (print production) Rita Sinha
Producers (pre-production)
Francesca Wardell, Rachel Ng
Publisher Andrew Macintyre

DK INDIA
Senior editor Priyanka Nath
Senior art editor Rajnish Kashyap
Assistant editor Deeksha Saikia
Assistant art editor Dhirendra Singh
Managing editor Alka Thakur Hazarika
Managing art editor Romi Chakraborty
DTP designer Anita Yadav
Picture researcher Sumedha Chopra

First published in Great Britain in 2003
This edition published in Great Britain in 2013
by Dorling Kindersley Limited
80 Strand, London WC2R 0RL

Copyright © 2003, © 2013 Dorling Kindersley Limited
A Penguin Company

13 14 15 16 17 10 9 8 7 6 5 4 3 2 1
001 – 192751 – 06/13

A CIP catalogue record for this book
is available from the British Library.

ISBN 978-1-4093-2836-0

Colour reproduction by Scanhouse, Malaysia
Printed and bound in China by Hung Hing

Discover more at
www.dk.com

Contents

Spitting fire

Deep inside the Earth, rocks melt into a thick liquid called magma. When the pressure in the Earth's crust builds up, it is magma that explodes out in a volcanic eruption.

As it rises, the magma breaks up rocks near the surface, which can cause earthquakes.

Hot rocks

The red-hot molten rock that explodes out of a volcano is beautiful but deadly. It is so hot that it can melt steel.

Earth's crust

The Earth's crust is made of... Loose rocks and dirt.

Sedimentary rocks made from bits of rock squashed together.

Igneous rocks made from magma that has cooled.

Metamorphic rocks made from squashed rocks.

Once it has risen to the surface, magma is called lava.

Ready to blow
The force of an exploding volcano can throw lava more than 610 m (2,000 ft) into the air. Ash can be thrown up to 40 km (25 miles) high!

Lower mantle

Outer core

Inner core

The Earth's crust is a layer of rock between 5.6 and 68 km (3.5 and 42 miles) thick.

The layer of moving rock below the crust is the mantle.

Peeling away the layers
The Earth is made up of many layers, just like an onion. Instead of onion skin, the Earth's layers are made of rock and metals.

Deep in the Earth
Below the mantle is the outer core. This layer is made up of iron and nickel that has melted. Below this is the inner core, where temperatures reach 4,500 °C (8,132 °F).

Jigsaw Earth

The Earth's crust is broken into pieces called plates, which are always moving. Sometimes we can feel the movement in an earthquake. Many volcanoes occur in places where plates bump together or pull apart.

North American Plate

The Ring of Fire circles the Pacific.

San Andreas Fault

Lanzarote, Canary Islands

Caribbean Plate

Cocos Plate

Pacific Plate

Nazca Plate

South American Plate

Scotia Plate

Antarctic Plate

Visible fault

The San Andreas Fault, in California, USA, is a place where two plates slide against each other. The plates move about 1 cm (0.5 in) a year.

All in a row

On Lanzarote, Canary Islands, magma bubbles up in places where plates break apart. These weak spots are called fissures.

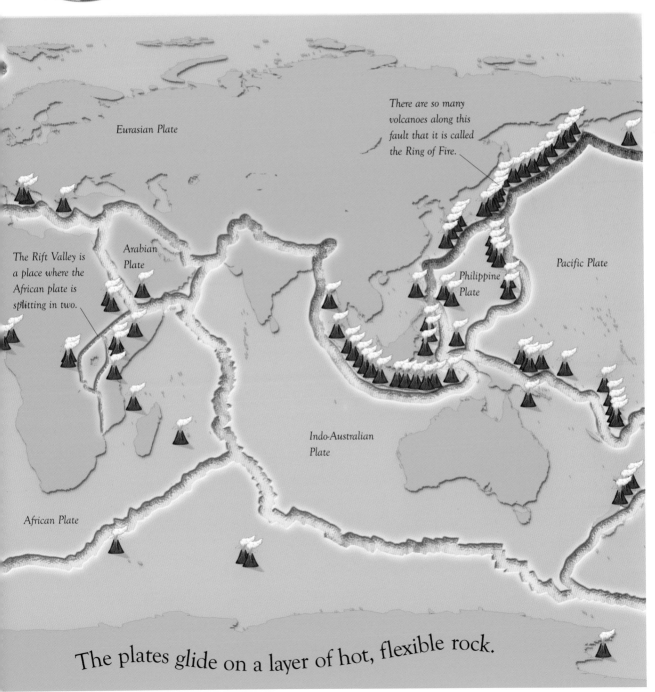

Eurasian Plate

There are so many volcanoes along this fault that it is called the Ring of Fire.

The Rift Valley is a place where the African plate is splitting in two.

Arabian Plate

Pacific Plate

Philippine Plate

African Plate

Indo-Australian Plate

The plates glide on a layer of hot, flexible rock.

Hot spots

In some places, the Earth's crust is thin enough for a column of hot magma to burn a hole and create a volcano. These places are called hot spots.

Hot water spot
Yellowstone Park in Wyoming, USA, is located over a hot spot. Two million years ago a volcano erupted here. Today, underground heat fuels the park's 10,000 geysers.

Lava erupts from Piton de la Fournaise in many places at the same time.

Island of fire
Réunion Island, in the Indian Ocean, contains one of the world's most active volcanoes – Piton de la Fournaise. Réunion Island formed over a hot spot about 5 million years ago.

North America

Yellowstone

Azores

Europe

Asia

Africa

South America

Réunion Island

Australia

Antarctic

In the ocean

The thin plates at the bottom of the sea are most easily pierced by hot magma. When this happens, an island is formed over the hot spot.

 Plate line

 Hot spot

Underground oven

The Azores islands lie over a hot spot in the Atlantic Ocean. People here take advantage of the free underground heat and use it to cook their food.

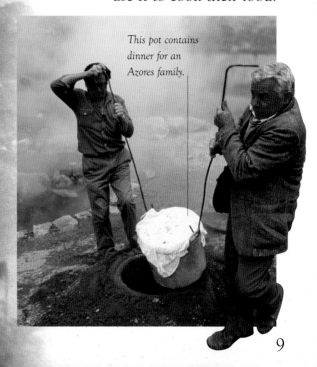

This pot contains dinner for an Azores family.

Red-hot rivers

When a volcano erupts, hot liquid rock either explodes outwards, or flows onto the Earth. Once it is outside the volcano, the liquid rock can cause a lot of damage.

Exploding ou

Sometimes, the liquid rock is unde a lot of pressure underground When this happens, the lava spurt or explodes out of the volcano

Destructive heat

Hot, liquid lava spreads out into rivers that can cover the countryside before it cools. It burns anything in its path, even roads.

Slow but steady

When lava seeps out of the ground rather than explodes, it travels very slowly. Flowing lava is easier to run away from than exploding lava, but it is just as destructive to the landscape.

Aa and Pahoehoe

There are many types of lava. Aa lava moves quickly and hardens to form sharp chunks. Pahoehoe lava moves slowly and often forms smooth rock when it hardens.

Aa rock is covered in sharp chunks and is difficult to walk over once it has cooled.

Pahoehoe lava flows grow a smooth skin.

Lava facts

● The temperature of some lava is seven to twelve times hotter than boiling water.

● The words "aa" and "pahoehoe" come from the Hawaiian language.

● Lava can form many different shapes, such as cones, tubes, and even strands as fine as hair!

As lava cools, it forms a hard "skin" over the liquid flow.

Glowing river

This intensely hot aa lava flow glows brightly. As it cools, the flow slows down and thickens, but since it cools very slowly, it can cover hundreds of kilometres before it stops.

Deadly blast

When a volcano explodes, gases inside the earth escape with so much force that the lava is blasted into billions of tiny pieces. These pieces of rock come in all sizes, from huge boulders to fine dust.

Inside this cloud of ash there may be pieces of rock, gravel, and dust.

Steamy beginning

Steam can sometimes be seen escaping from the top or sides of a volcano. This is often the first sign that a volcano is active or may be getting ready to erupt.

Poisonous gas

Rocks and lava are dangerous, but the most deadly types of eruptions spew out tonnes of ash an poisonous gases that can cause death by suffocation

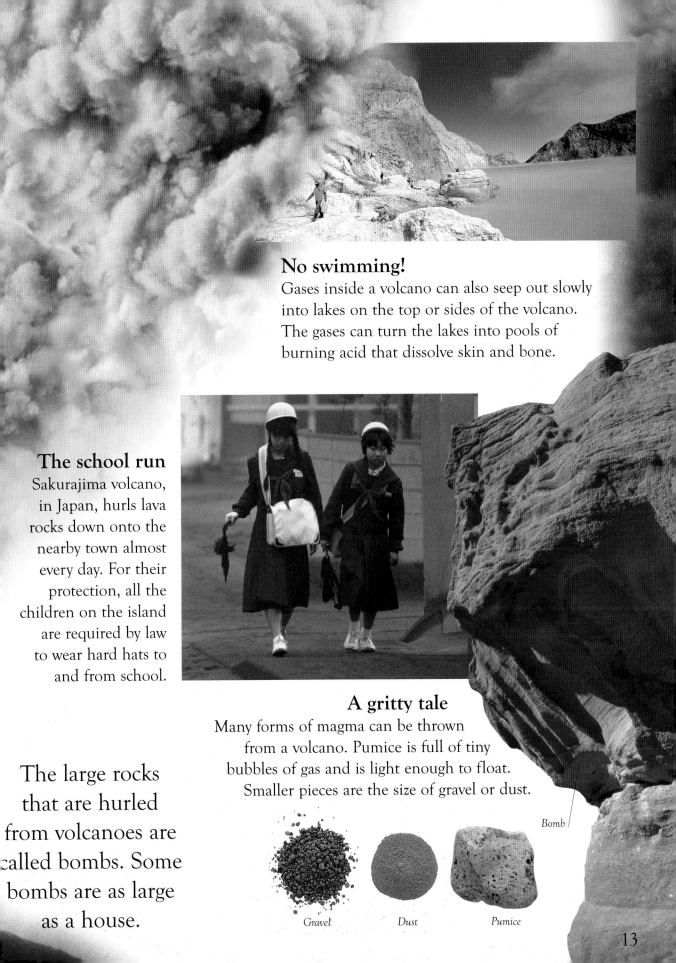

No swimming!

Gases inside a volcano can also seep out slowly into lakes on the top or sides of the volcano. The gases can turn the lakes into pools of burning acid that dissolve skin and bone.

The school run

Sakurajima volcano, in Japan, hurls lava rocks down onto the nearby town almost every day. For their protection, all the children on the island are required by law to wear hard hats to and from school.

A gritty tale

Many forms of magma can be thrown from a volcano. Pumice is full of tiny bubbles of gas and is light enough to float. Smaller pieces are the size of gravel or dust.

Bomb

The large rocks that are hurled from volcanoes are called bombs. Some bombs are as large as a house.

Gravel

Dust

Pumice

Volcanic weather

When a volcano erupts, huge amounts of dust and ash are thrown high up into the atmosphere. This debris can affect the weather all over the world, blocking out sunlight and turning summer days cold.

Travelling ash

This satellite photo was taken in 1991, one month after Mt Pinatubo erupted in the Philippines. The light areas show the ash and dust from the volcano. It had already spread all around the world.

The eruption of Mt Pinatubo lowered world temperatures by 0.5°C (1°F) for one year.

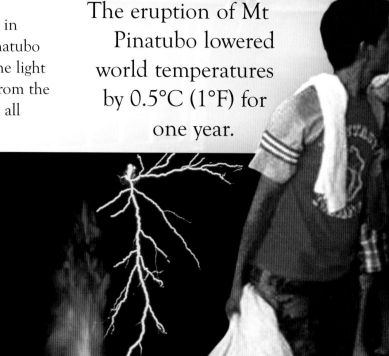

Lightning strikes

Lightning is often seen during eruptions. It is caused by tiny pieces of lava in an ash cloud rubbing against each other. The rubbing creates an electrical charge, which is lightning.

14

Turning day to night
When Mt Pinatubo erupted,
clouds of ash 40 km
(25 miles) high blocked out
the Sun. The land was dark
and covered with grey ash.

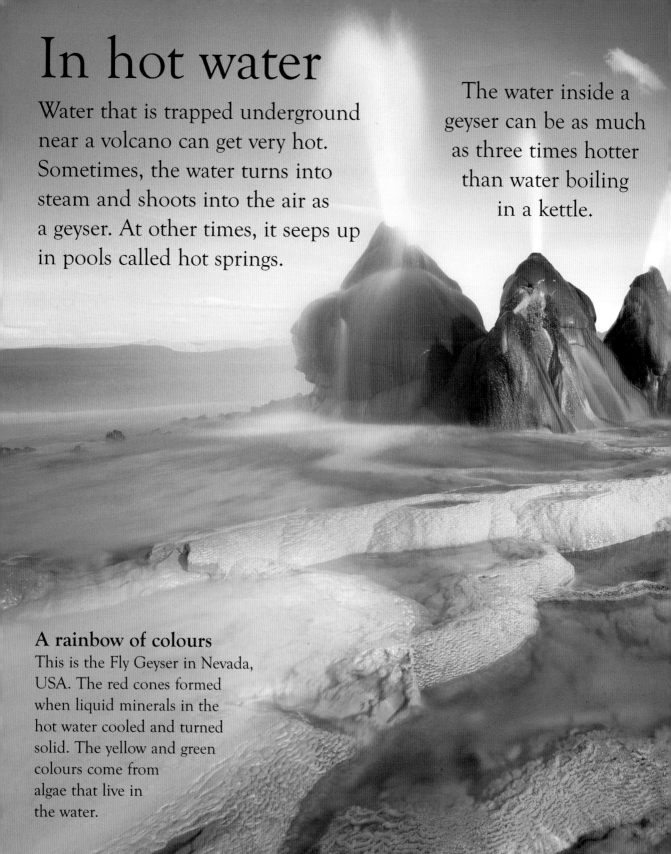

In hot water

Water that is trapped underground near a volcano can get very hot. Sometimes, the water turns into steam and shoots into the air as a geyser. At other times, it seeps up in pools called hot springs.

The water inside a geyser can be as much as three times hotter than water boiling in a kettle.

A rainbow of colours
This is the Fly Geyser in Nevada, USA. The red cones formed when liquid minerals in the hot water cooled and turned solid. The yellow and green colours come from algae that live in the water.

Glorious mud

Underground heat from a volcano can
even boil mud. This mud is rich in
minerals and is often collected and used
as a skin treatment. People bathe in the
mud to make their skin soft and smooth.

*Old Faithful shoots
water between 30 and
50 m (98–165 ft) into
the air.*

Old Faithful

One of the most popular
geysers in the world is
Old Faithful in Yellowstone
National Park, USA.
This geyser spurts faithfully
every 78 minutes or so.

Fire under the sea

Under the sea, hot magma, chemicals, and minerals burn their way through thin spots in the Earth's plates. The lava and minerals bubble up to make islands and other unusual homes for undersea life.

Studying a hot subject

When lava erupts in water, it moves slowly and cools quickly. Scientists study underwater lava flows to learn more about how islands form.

LAVA DIVING

Because magma cools down quickly underwater, experienced scuba divers can sometimes get a close-up look at small, undersea eruptions.

Underwater chimneys

The minerals that rise to the ocean floor from deep in the Earth sometimes harden and make a chimney shape. These chimneys are called black smokers. Many unusual animals live in the warm, mineral waters.

Black smoker facts

● Most black smokers are more than 2 km (1 mile) below the surface.

● The first black smoker was discovered in 1977.

● The animals living near black smokers include mussels, clams, and crabs.

Living on a chimney

Colourful tube worms live around black smokers. Special bacteria live inside these worms. They change the chemicals pouring out of the smokers into food.

This crab has made its home on the tube worms.

The volcanic seabed

Scientists believe there may be as many as 20,000 volcanoes under the sea. That's more than 90 per cent of all the volcanoes on the planet. Many of the Earth's islands were formed from these undersea volcanoes.

This extinct volcano has stopped erupting.

An active volcano about to erupt under the ocean floor

19

Birth of an island

When a volcano erupts deep under the sea, the lava piles up instead of flowing away. If the eruptions continue, the lava gradually builds up, until one day it breaks the surface and forms an island.

An island's birthday
In 1963, fishermen near Iceland saw a new island rise out of the water. The island was named Surtsey, after Surtur, the ancient Norse god of fire.

Three years later...
Once the lava flows stopped, plants and animals began to find their way to the new island. After just a few years, Surtsey was home to birds, grasses, and seals.

It takes millions of years for a volcano to reach the surface and become an island.

Underwater laboratory
As a new volcano grows towards the surface, it provides a home for a wide variety of marine life. This is why growing volcanoes are a great place to study undersea life.

Islands may look large, but they are only a tiny bit of the whole volcano.

Home, sweet home

The Galápagos Islands, in the Pacific Ocean, are volcanic islands that broke the surface of the water about 4 million years ago. Since that time, many types of animals and plants have come to live on the islands.

Tsunami

Many coastal towns' worst dread is a tsunami – a huge wave that destroys everything in its path. Many tsunamis are caused by volcanic eruptions.

Making waves
When a volcano erupts under the sea, large parts of the ocean floor are lifted up, displacing water and creating a wave.

Landslide danger
Tsunamis are also caused when a large eruption sends huge amounts of lava and mud tumbling into the ocean

At first, the displaced water is almost invisible as it travels quickly towards the shore.

A tsunami starts when a volcano erupts on the ocean floor.

Far out at sea, lava deep inside the Earth rises to the surface.

Tsunamis can travel up to 805 kph (500 mph) at sea.

Dangerous wave

Tsunamis can be even more dangerous than the eruptions that cause them. One of the deadliest tsunamis of all time was the 2004 Indian Ocean tsunami, though this was caused by a massive undersea earthquake and not a volcanic eruption.

City threatened

Huge tsunamis can sweep away entire towns and villages, flood hundreds of metres inland, and strip away beaches and vegetation.

When the tsunami reaches shallow water, it swells upwards, forming a huge wave.

Water travelling back from the shore is also sucked up into the wave. A towering and terrifying tsunami is about to hit land!

Tsunami facts

● On 21 May 1792, Unzen volcano caused a tsunami that killed 14,300 people.

● The tallest recorded tsunami was 85 m (279 ft) high.

● The word tsunami means "harbour wave" in Japanese.

Dead or alive?

Some volcanoes can seem to be dead, but they are only sleeping. A volcano that is not erupting, but might erupt again, is called dormant. A volcano that cannot erupt any more is called extinct.

In the shadow of Mt Fuji

Mt Fuji, in Japan, has been dormant since 1770, but could come to life again at any time. This would be devastating for the 12 million people of Tokyo – 97 km (60 miles) away.

Out of the blue

Mt Pinatubo, in the Philippines, erupted in 1991 after lying dormant for 400 years. Ash and gas flowed along the ground faster than a car. The driver of this blue truck had to really put his foot down to escape.

WAKING UP

Mt Pinatubo began waking up in April 1991, when people heard rumbling sounds and saw steam and ash coming from the sides of the volcano. More than 200,000 people were quickly evacuated from the area. The volcano finally erupted in mid-July.

Starting to wake up

Scientists use satellites to keep a close watch on dormant volcanoes. The dots on these photos of Chiliques volcano, in Chile, show where magma is rising as the volcano wakes up.

Infrared image of Chiliques volcano

Satellite image of Chiliques volcano

On solid ground

This church in Le Puy, in France, was built on the remains of an old volcano. The volcano is extinct and will never erupt again.

Living in fear

Mount Etna, in Italy, is Europe's largest and most active volcano. The volcano has erupted at least 190 times in 3,500 years, but even so, thousands of people live and work on its slopes.

Blast from the past

One of the most dramatic eruptions of Mt Etna was in 1669. Fifteen villages around the volcano were buried by lava, but no one was killed.

A pet's sixth sense

Some people who live near Mt Etna watch the behaviour of their pet cats to try and predict eruptions. Cats are very sensitive to changes in pressure that occur just before an eruption.

A constant threat

When Mt Etna erupted in 2002, people living near the volcano were evacuated as the lava got close. It has erupted several times since then.

Early warning systems around Mt Etna help people escape in time.

Build a barrier

The people living near Mt Etna build barriers to help divert the flow of lava away from populated areas. During the 1669 eruption, the people of one town used rocks to divert the lava. Today, mechanical diggers are used.

Luckily, Mt Etna's lava flows very slowly.

Lava-land

There are more than 200 volcanoes in Iceland, which lies over a large hot spot in the Earth's crust. In January 1973, Eldfell volcano, on the island of Heimaey, erupted. The eruption continued for six months.

A curtain of fire

During the eruption of Eldfell, lava fountains spurted up from cracks in the volcano and formed a curtain of fire. Seawater was used to cool the lava and slow down the flow.

Buried homes

Most of Heimaey's 5,300 inhabitants were taken to Iceland's mainland and so escaped the eruption. Most of the island's buildings, however, were buried in black ash. Many of the buildings were later dug out and restored.

Eldfell means "fire mountain" in Icelandic. This fire mountain buried or destroyed more than 370 buildings

A massive eruption

In March 2010, Eyjafjallajökull volcano, Iceland's sixth largest glacier, erupted. The eruption continued over a few months. It disrupted air traffic across Europe for several weeks and affected many people and businesses around the world.

A natural heat

The heat from Iceland's many volcanoes is put to good use. People bathe and relax in hot pools like this one, while the nearby power plant uses the heat from the water to make electricity.

Mount Saint Helens

One of the best-studied eruptions of all time occurred on 18 May 1980. That morning, Mt St Helens, in the state of Washington, USA, exploded in a fury of ash and smoke while scientists nearby took measurements.

Before 1980 eruption

After 1980 eruption

Blowing its top

Before the eruption, Mt St Helens had a beautiful snow-capped peak. The blast tore off most of the north side of the volcano and left a huge, gaping hole big enough to fit an entire city into. This was the first time scientists had ever watched a volcano erupt from its side.

Huge explosion

Rocks, ash, volcanic gas, and steam blasted upwards and outwards faster than a jet plane and hotter than a furnace. Ash rose 24 km (15 miles) into the atmosphere in just 15 minutes.

The top 400 m (1,312 ft) of Mt St Helens was blasted away.

A dreadful aftermath
The blast killed 57 people, destroyed wildlife and river valleys, and knocked down enough trees to build 300,000 homes.

A bottle of ash, please!
Ash from the eruption blocked out the sunlight for 400 km (250 miles) around. Later, the ash was bottled up and sold as a souvenir.

Montserrat

The tiny island of Montserrat in the Caribbean was very peaceful until 1995. That year, Soufriere Hills volcano began erupting. Most of the residents had to flee the island in fear of their lives.

Paradise regained

Montserrat was once a popular holiday spot. For a long time after the eruption the airport was buried under ash, and tourists had to arrive by ferry, but life is now returning to normal.

Buried and deserted

In December 1997, Montserrat's capital city, Plymouth, was buried in 2 m (6 ft) of mud and ash.

Time to rebuild

Some buildings, like this bell tower, survived the 1995 eruption and were dug out, but following the eruption in 1997, Plymouth was abandoned. A new capital, Little Bay, is now being developed.

Squeezed out
The people of Montserrat have been squeezed into smaller and smaller parts of their island as the volcano has taken over. There is now a large exclusion zone. The new capital of Little Bay is being developed in the northwest of the island.

Plymouth, former capital city

Little Bay

This area is the only part considered safe to live on.

Montserrat facts

● Around 8,000 people, two-thirds of the population, have left the island.

● Scientists think the Soufriere Hills volcano is about 100,000 years old.

● Since 1995, the eruptions have killed 20 people.

Land of fire

Indonesia lies in between two large plates. It is home to over 125 active volcanoes and has more recorded eruptions than any other country. Many of Indonesia's 15,000 islands were formed by volcanic activity.

Big bang
When Krakatau volcano erupted in 1883, the explosion was heard 4,000 km (2,400 miles) away at Alice Springs in Australia.

A beauty and a beast
Tengger Caldera is one of Indonesia's most visited volcanic areas. Its beauty masks a fiery heart – there have been more than 50 eruptions here in the last 200 years. It last erupted in 2011.

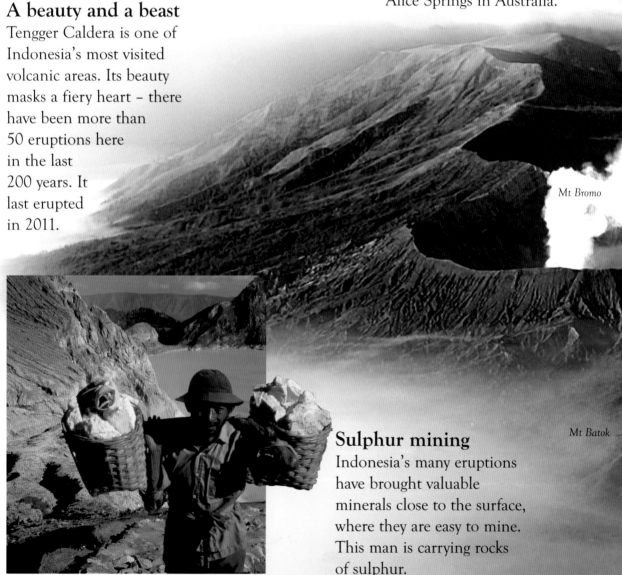

Mt Bromo

Mt Batok

Sulphur mining
Indonesia's many eruptions have brought valuable minerals close to the surface, where they are easy to mine. This man is carrying rocks of sulphur.

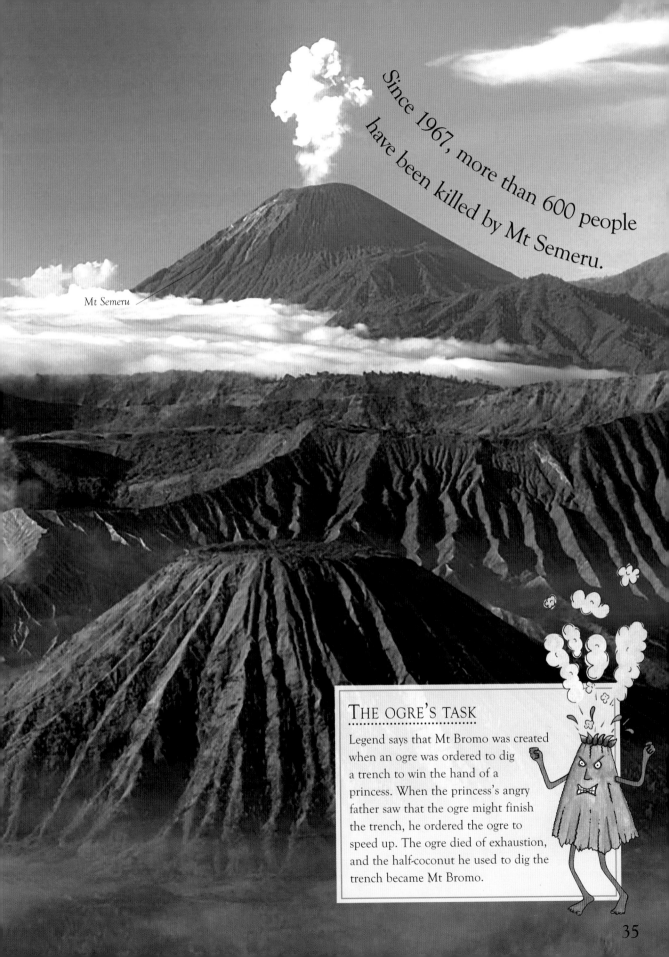

Since 1967, more than 600 people have been killed by Mt Semeru.

Mt Semeru

THE OGRE'S TASK

Legend says that Mt Bromo was created when an ogre was ordered to dig a trench to win the hand of a princess. When the princess's angry father saw that the ogre might finish the trench, he ordered the ogre to speed up. The ogre died of exhaustion, and the half-coconut he used to dig the trench became Mt Bromo.

Ancient tragedy

On the morning of 24 August, 79 CE, Mt Vesuvius, in Italy, erupted. Hot ash, dust, lava, and clouds of deadly gas rained down on the people of Pompeii and Herculaneum, burying both the towns for 1,600 years.

Preserved in ash

Pompeii is so well preserved that it provides us with good evidence of everyday life in an ancient Roman town. Archaeologists can even read the graffiti on the town's walls.

A Pompeiian victim

This man suffocated in the smoke and ash of the eruption. His body later decayed to leave a hole. In modern times, the hole was filled with plaster to make a cast.

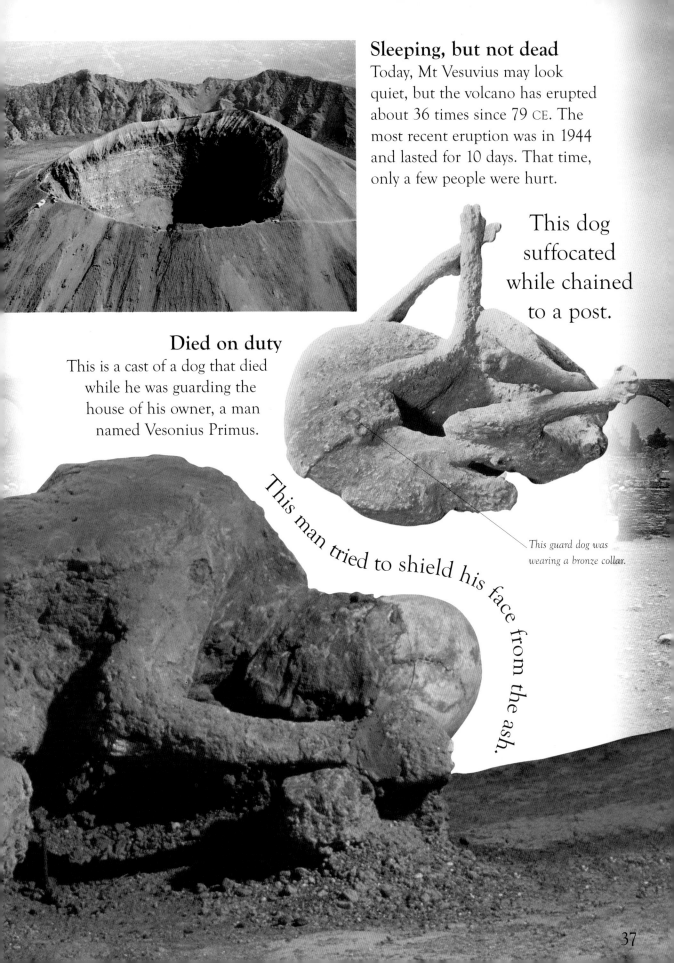

Sleeping, but not dead

Today, Mt Vesuvius may look quiet, but the volcano has erupted about 36 times since 79 CE. The most recent eruption was in 1944 and lasted for 10 days. That time, only a few people were hurt.

This dog suffocated while chained to a post.

Died on duty

This is a cast of a dog that died while he was guarding the house of his owner, a man named Vesonius Primus.

This guard dog was wearing a bronze collar.

This man tried to shield his face from the ash.

37

Work in the hot zone

A scientist who studies volcanoes is called a volcanologist. For these scientists, research can get pretty hot. In order to collect information about volcanoes, they must get close to a volcano's fiery interior.

Suited and booted

To pick up burning rock samples and walk across red-hot lava, volcanologists need to wear special suits and heat-proof boots.

The silver suit reflects the heat of the volcano and leaves the person inside cool.

DANGEROUS WORK

When volcanologists work around an active volcano, if there is any warning of an eruption or violent activity, they usually leave. Unfortunately, sometimes the activity changes quickly and there is little or no warning. A number of volcanologists have died while studying volcanoes.

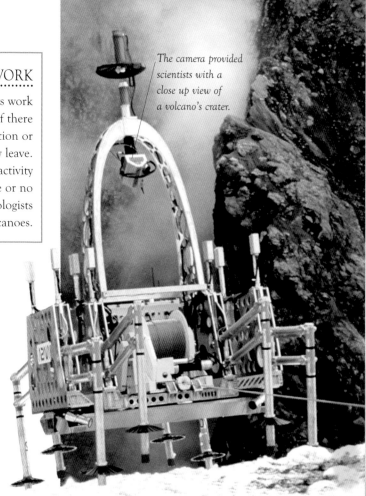

The camera provided scientists with a close up view of a volcano's crater.

Robot on a mission

The Dante robot was once sent into volcanoes to gather information from places it was too dangerous for people to go. Its mission ended abruptly when it crashed during an expedition to a volcano in Antarctica.

These volcanologists are taking samples of gas. The gas may give clues as to when the volcano will next erupt.

Deadly gases

Even if it is not too hot, there may be invisible dangers in the form of deadly gases seeping from below ground. This is why gas masks are required equipment for volcanologists.

Visiting a volcano

Volcanoes are fascinating, and many people will go a long way to visit them. Each year, thousands of tourists travel to active volcanoes for the opportunity to get up close and personal with boiling lava.

Popular volcanoes

- Erta Ale, in Ethiopia, has erupted nonstop from 1967.

- Yasur volcano in Vanuatu has erupted 10–20 times each hour for 800 years.

- Tourists to White Island volcano in New Zealand can walk right inside the crater.

It's safer up here

Some volcanoes can only be safely visited from the air. Hot lava and poisonous gases make it too dangerous to get any closer. These volcanoes are best toured by helicopter.

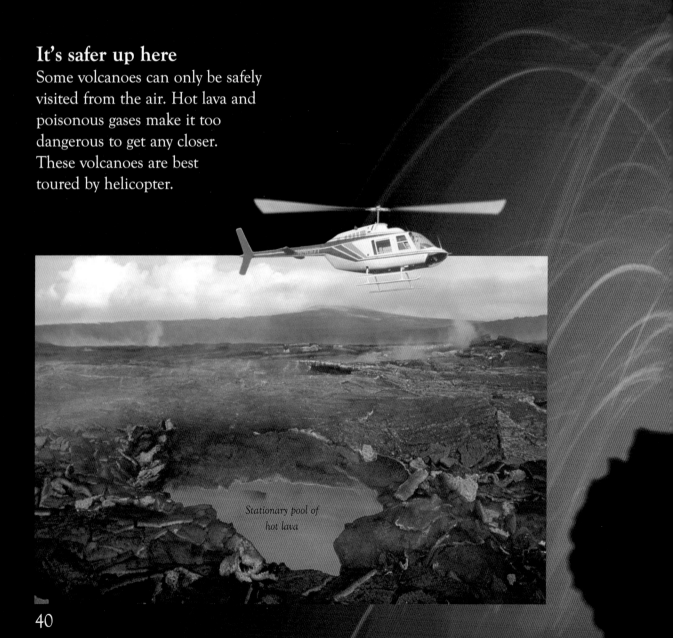

Stationary pool of hot lava

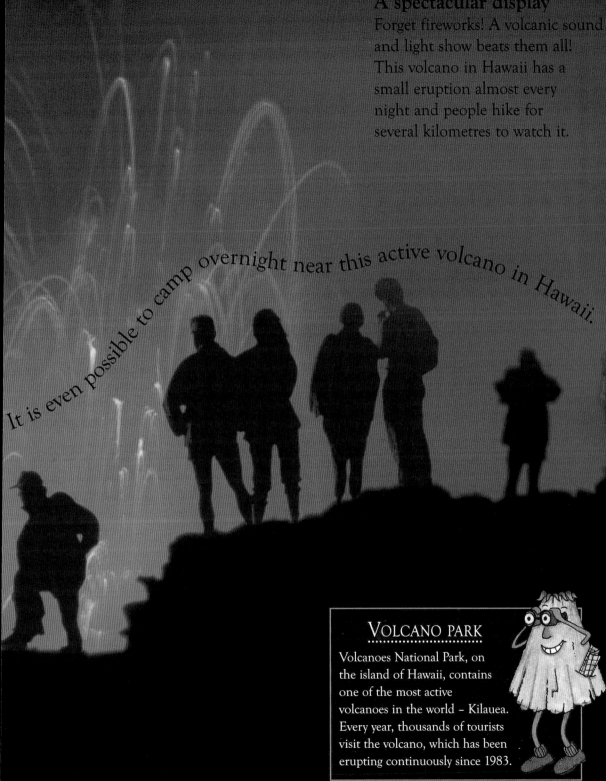

A spectacular display

Forget fireworks! A volcanic sound and light show beats them all! This volcano in Hawaii has a small eruption almost every night and people hike for several kilometres to watch it.

It is even possible to camp overnight near this active volcano in Hawaii.

VOLCANO PARK
....

Volcanoes National Park, on the island of Hawaii, contains one of the most active volcanoes in the world – Kilauea. Every year, thousands of tourists visit the volcano, which has been erupting continuously since 1983.

Weird and wonderful

Lava flows can form a large variety of weird and wonderful shapes when they cool. Sometimes, even scientists cannot explain how all these fantastic features were created!

Towering cones of lava
These structures in Pinnacles National Park, California, USA, were formed 7,700 years ago by lava erupting from nearby Mt Mazama.

Chimney houses

Hundreds of years ago, people hollowed out these volcanic chimneys in Cappadocia, Turkey, and used them as houses. People still live in some of them.

A road for giants

The people of ancient Ireland believed these rocks were the work of a giant named Finn McCool. The Giant's Causeway was actually created 60 million years ago by cooling lava flows.

Time to warm up

These Japanese monkeys have learnt that a soak in a nearby volcanic hot spring makes a nice break from the winter chill and helps them to stay clean.

Animals also enjoy unusual volcanic areas.

Out of the ashes

Volcanic eruptions can bring
devastation, but they can also
bring renewal. Eruptions clear out
old, dead plants, while the ash
helps plants grow back more
quickly and stronger than before.

Life returns
A few years after an eruption,
plant life has returned to
this volcano. The ash
helps the plants
grow quickly.

First sign of growth
Ferns are some of the first plants
to grow after an eruption. They
have very tough seeds and are
able to push their way up
through solid lava.

ertile slopes

olcanic ash makes a great
rtilizer to help plants grow.
armers near this volcano in
ndonesia take advantage of
is by growing their crops all
e way up the sides and
 to the crater of
is volcano.

Making a meal of it

Without volcanoes, many people
who live in some of the poorest
places in the world would struggle
to grow enough food. The ash
makes poor farm land fertile
enough to feed everyone.

Path to safety

Find a safe path through the hot lava by answering the questions correctly. Watch your step!

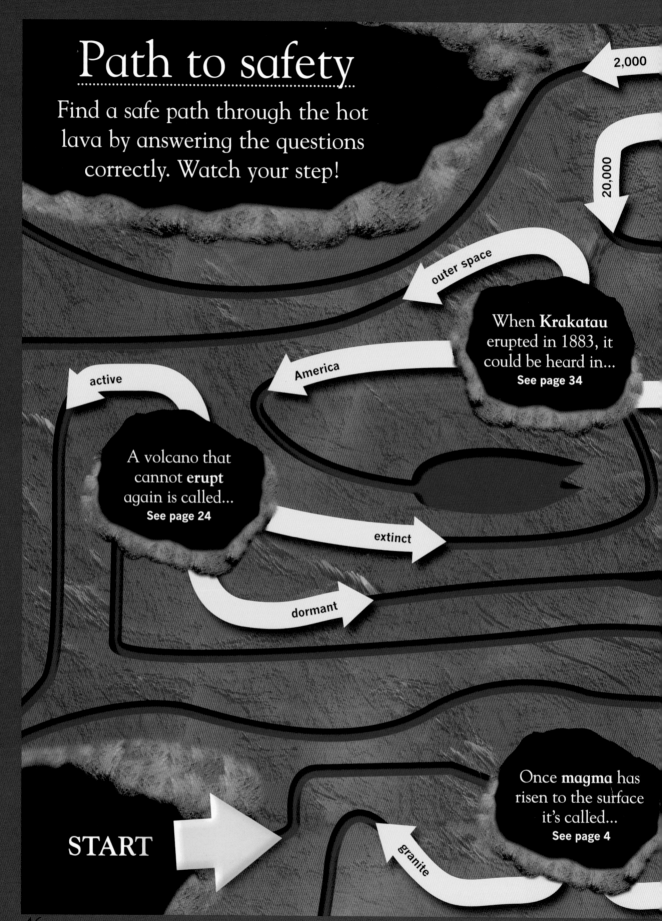

2,000

20,000

outer space

America

active

extinct

dormant

When **Krakatau** erupted in 1883, it could be heard in...
See page 34

A volcano that cannot **erupt** again is called...
See page 24

Once **magma** has risen to the surface it's called...
See page 4

granite

START

The **number** of
volcanoes in Iceland
is more than...
See page 28

FINISH

200

tsunamis

geysers

Australia

the same as the air outside

hotter than boiling water

colder than ice

Huge waves
caused by **eruptions**
are called...
See page 22

ash clouds

lava

The **temperature**
of some lava is...
See page 11

oal

47

True or false?

How much have you learned about volcanoes? Can you spot which of these statements are true and which are false?

Mt Etna is Europe's smallest and least active volcano.
See pages 26–27

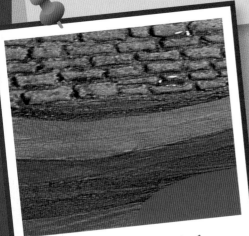

Igneous rocks are made from magma that has cooled.
See page 4

The Ring of Fire circles the Indian Ocean.
See pages 6–7

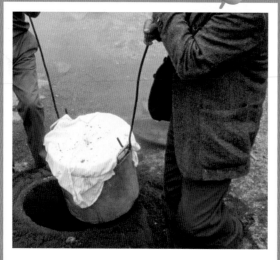

People in the Azores islands take advantage of the underground heat and use it to cook their food.
See page 9

When lava seeps out of the ground instead of exploding, it travels very fast.
See page 10

The lava collected from Mt Saint Helens eruption was bottled up and sold as a souvenir.
See page 31

Volcanologists wear special suits to keep warm.
See page 38

It takes about five years for a volcano to reach the surface and become an island.
See pages 20–21

Monkeys bathe in volcanic hot springs.
See page 43

Plants can push their way up through solid lava to grow back.
See page 44

The Old Faithful geyser in USA spurts every 78 minutes or so.
See page 17

Picture quiz

Are you hot on volcanoes? Test yourself with this quiz. All the answers can be found in the book.

A scientist who studies volcanoes.
See page 38

This is the name given to magma once it rises to the surface. It is so hot, it can melt steel.
See page 4

This slow moving kind of lava forms a smooth rock when it hardens.
See page 10

These are made from rocks squashed together.
See page 4

These are created from magma that has cooled.
See page 4

This forms when a volcano explodes and gases inside the Earth escape. It contains pieces of rock, gravel, and dust.
See page 12

Tourists to the White Island volcano in New Zealand can walk right inside this part of the volcano.
See page 40

This is a fast moving kind of lava. When it hardens, it forms sharp rocks.
See page 10

This layer of Earth is made of loose rocks and dirt. It is 5.6–68 km (3.5–42 miles) thick.
See pages 4–5

This is a thick liquid made of melted rocks, deep inside the Earth.
See page 4

These are made from bits of rock squashed together.
See page 4

What's this?

Take a look at these close-ups
of the pictures in the book, and
see if you can identify them.
The clues should help you!

- This volcano has erupted
  190 times in 3,500 years.
- Thousands of people
  work on its slopes.

See pages 26–27

- The ash collected from
  this volcano was sold
  as a souvenir.
- It erupted from its side.

See pages 30–31

- He suffocated in the
  smoke and ash of
  an eruption.
- His body decayed to
  leave a hole.

See pages 36–37

- It is named after the
  ancient Norse god
  of fire.
- It rose out of the water
  in 1963.

See page 20

- This was sent into
  volcanoes to gather
  information.
- It crashed on a visit to
  a volcano in Antarctica.

See page 39

- This underground heat
  fuels 10,000 geysers.
- A volcano erupted here
  two million years ago.

See page 8

People used to believe that a giant named Finn McCool created this.

It was actually created by cooling lava flows.

See page 43

This is located in the USA.

This is where two plates slide against each other.

See page 7

It is difficult to walk over it once it has cooled.

It moves quickly and hardens to form sharp chunks.

See page 10

It has erupted 36 times since 79 CE.

This volcano is in Italy.

See pages 36–37

People watch their behaviour to predict eruptions.

They are sensitive to changes in pressure.

See page 26

Animals such as mussels, clams, and crabs live near them.

The first one was discovered in 1977.

See page 19

Glossary

Here are the meanings of some words that are useful to know when learning about volcanoes.

Aa lava a crumbly, lumpy type of lava that moves slowly and can form tall flows.

Algae small, simple plants that live in water.

Ash very small, fine particles of lava that can block out sunlight.

Bacteria microscopic animals that can get their energy from chemicals.

Basalt the most common kind of volcanic rock, made from very runny lava.

Black smoker volcanic vent on the sea floor that belches out hot minerals.

Bomb big blob of lava that is thrown out by a volcano and cools in mid-air.

Chemical a natural substance made when different types of atoms combine together.

Core the metallic centre of the Earth.

Crater the part of a volcano that connects to the main chimney and out of which lava and ash erupts.

Crater lake a lake formed in the crater of a volcano.

Crust the hard, outer layer of the Earth.

rmant a volcano that has
erupted for a long time,
could erupt again.

ıption when lava, ash, or
explodes out of a volcano.

tinct a volcano that cannot
r erupt again.

ılt a crack in the Earth's
ıst where rocks have moved.

sure a crack in the ground
ich runny lava oozes out of.

yser a place where
derground water, heated by
gma, spurts into the air.

t spot a place where rising
gma burns through the
rth's crust.

Hot spring a place where hot
water from under the ground
bubbles to the surface.

Landslide the sliding of
loose earth and rock down
a steep slope.

Lava the name for magma that
has erupted to the surface.

Magma rock deep in the Earth
that has melted to a liquid.

Mantle the part of the Earth's
interior that lies in between
the crust and the core.

Metamorphic rock rock
formed from other rocks
that are under intense heat
and pressure.

Mineral a natural substance
that is not a plant or animal.

Mud pot a pool of hot,
boiling mud.

Pahoehoe lava a hot, runny
lava that moves freely in
shallow flows.

Plate the moving part of the
mantle and crust.

Rift a place where two plates
are pulling apart to create a
crack in the crust.

Ring of Fire an area in the
Pacific Ocean that includes
many of the world's most
active and violent volcanoes.

Seismograph a machine that
measures the movement of the
Earth's surface.

Tsunami a destructive sea
wave that can be caused by
a volcanic eruption.

Volcanologist a scientist who
studies volcanoes.

Index

Acknowledgements

Dorling Kindersley would like to thank:
Colin Bowler of Alan Collinson Design/Geo-Innovations, for map design, and Louise Halsey for her original volcano illustrations. Thanks, also, to the following DK staff: Jacqueline Gooden, Elinor Greenwood, Lorrie Mack, Fleur Star, Cheryl Telfer, and Sadie Thomas.

Picture credits

The publisher would like to thank the following for their kind permission to reproduce their photographs:
(Key: a-above; b-below/bottom; c-centre; f-far; l-left; r-right; t-top)

Mario Cipollini 27tl; **Bruce Coleman Inc:** Stella Sneered 20cr; **Corbis:** 26-27c, 58crb; James Balog/Aurora Photos 59clb (Volcano watching); G. Brad Lewis/Science Faction 58tc (Bubbling Lava); **Image Plan** 59ca; Michael S. Lewis 52br; Yann Arthus-Bertrand 43b, 44-45, 49cr, 59; Dan Bool/Sygma 34-35; Gary Braasch 31br; Carol Cohen 44c, 49bl; Sergio Dorantes 34tr; Chris Hellier 43tl; Ted Horowitz 44l; Michael S. Lewis 8tr; Ludovic Maisant 13tr; Pat O'Hara 42, 48; Robert Patrick 32tr, 32bl; Roger Ressmeyer 13c, 20bl, 36-37b, 39b, 40bl, 41b, 41t, 52c; Hans Georg Roth 9br, 48bl; **Royalty-Free Images** 24tr; Sean Sexton 37cr; Strauss/Curtis 45br; Kevin Schafer 44bl; Hans Strand 29cr; James A Sugar 31br; Nick Wheeler 22c; Ralph White 19cr, 53bl; Adam Woolfit 25cr; **Ecoscene:** Wayne Lawler 48c; Lin Esposito: 36c; **GeoScience Features Picture Library:** 20tl; **Dreamstime.com:** Lucafabbian 53tl; **Dorling Kindersley:** Andy Crawford/Donks Models-modelmaker 58clb, **Museo Archeologico Nazionale di Napoli** 58cla (Cast of volcano victim), 59cla (Cast of volc victim), 59cb; **Natural History Museum, London** 58tc (Aa Rock), 58c 58c, 59clb (Volcanic bomb), 59bc; **Rough Guides** 58cla (Extinct volca 58cra, 58crb (Hot mud pool), 58crb (Volcano, Chile), 59tl, 59tr, 59ca (Cooling lava), 59cra, 59cra (Cooling lava); **The Science Museum, London** 58clb (Igneous rock); **Getty Images:** Barcroft Media 29tr, G. Brad Lewis/The Image Bank 48br; Tom Pfeiffer/VolcanoDiscovery/ Photographer's Choice 52tr, 53br, 58cb; Astromujoff/Riser 49cl; Warren Bolster 22-23c; Michael Dunning 22tr; Jack Dykinga 16-17; G. Brad Lewis 10cr, 46-47; **NASA** 21c; Guido Alberto Rossi 12cl; Schafer & Hill 22l; Pete Turner 28-29, 29tr; Greg Vaughn 2-3; **Art W** 12-13c; **Robert Harding Picture Library:** 10tr, 10cl, 11; **Photri** 30cl; E. Simanor 43tr; Katz/FSP: 14cl, 24-25; R. Gaillarde/Gamma 8-9; **NASA:** 5tr, 25tl, 25tc, 33tr; **Photoshot:** Stella Snead 52bl; Panos Pictur Rob Huibers 32-33; Chris and Helen Pellant: 17tl; **Popperfoto:** Tony Gentile/Reuters 1; Reuters 38; **Powerstock Photolibrary:** Superstock 13br; **Reuters:** Mario Laporta 49tr, 50cl; **Rex Features:** Sipa Press 15; **Science Photo Library:** 30-31; Bernhard Edmaier 2tc, 4-5c, 7tr, 34bl; NASA/Carnegie Mellon University 39tr, 52cl, 52bc; Mark Newman 14bc; David Parker 7tl, 53tc; **Seapics.com:** Doug Perrine 18; Verena Tunnicliffe: 19tr; **US Geological Survey:** Lyn Topinka, United States Department of the Interior, U.S Geological Survey, David A. Johnston Cascades Volcano Observatory, Vancouver, Washington 30cr.

All other images © Dorling Kindersley
For further information see: www.dkimages.com

Sulphur crystal

Aa rock

Bubbling lava

Lava flow

Melted nails

Cast of volcano victim

Extinct volcano

Firehole Lake Drive, USA

Basaltic lava

Crater Lake

Volcano, Chile

Volcano cross-section

Pahoehoe lava

Old Faithful geyser

Mt Rainier

Old Faithful geyser

Igneous rock

Mt Etna

Hot mud pool

Remains of dead trees

Cone-shaped hill

Inside a volcano

Volcanic ash

Volcano, Chile

Pumice

Lake in crater

Poás Volcano Park, Costa Rica

Extinct volcano

Crater of Mt Vesuvius

Lava flow into sea

Mt Kilimanjaro

Cast of volcano victim

Mt Fuji

The Blue Lagoon, Iceland

Stromboli volcano, Italy

Cooling lava

Burned forests

Cooling lava

Volcano watching

Volcano, Chile

Volcano victims

Mt Etna

Volcano, Hawaii

Volcanic bomb

Loburu hot springs

Earth's layers

Geyser, New Zealand

Bathing monkeys

Lava stalagmite

Volcano, Chile